I0140068

Divine Woman
by Design

Divine Woman
by Design

Written by
Kimberly L. Jordan & Margaret Parker

Copyright

©2018 Kimberly L Jordan and Margaret Parker. All rights reserved.

No part of this book may be reproduced in any written, electronic, recording, or photocopying without written permission of the publisher or author. The exception would be in the case of brief quotations embodied in the critical articles or reviews and pages where permission is specifically granted by the publisher or author.

Holy Bible Scriptures found in NIV, KJV, NKJV and CEV.

Books may be purchased by contacting the publisher or the author.

Cover Design: Ministering Moments
Editor: Ingrid Zacharias
Publisher: Butterfly Typeface Publishing
10515 W Markham St, Suite E6
Little Rock, Arkansas 72205

www.butterflytypeface.com

ISBN: 978-1-947656-05-5
ISBN10: 1947656058

1. Religion 2. Self-Help 3. Life Style 4. Spirituality

First Edition
Printed in the United States

Butterfly Typeface

Dedication

Kimberly and I would like to dedicate this book to women. It is our belief that from our experiences and from our heart we can reach you where you have not been reached before because it all started with us reaching each other – women. Information is power and sharing this information with you has been a very powerful thing for us. Share it forward.

Table of Contents

Foreword

In the New Testament we read that Jesus two thousand years ago released his disciples who accompanied him in ministry two by two among at least seventy-two others who preached and taught with him to minister the good news of Christ Consciousness throughout the territories of ancient Israel. Perhaps, many of them were women! The gospel of Luke says many women who traveled with him ministered to him from their substance.

This book written by two women who understand the culture and the religion that birthed Judaism and ultimately Christianity is a classic example of that ancient principle used by Jesus of sending two of his disciples together for a special mission.

The Creator has chosen and anointed two women who are; in my opinion, uniquely qualified to address Christ Consciousness from their own perspective based upon their separate individual experiences. Let this mind or this consciousness be in you which was in Jesus was the fascinating advice of the biblical apostle Paul! Christ Consciousness is a belief that every human is a measure of the Creator who created them whether they know it or not. Every human has a measure of the Creator's omnipotence, omniscience, and omnipresence. We are the exact image and likeness of God. We are spirit using a soul to create our reality and experiencing that reality with physical bodies.

This measure of Spirit present in a female is called the sacred divine! The Sacred Divine or the Divine Feminine or the Eternal Spirit hiding in every woman has always been a controversial subject since Mary Magdalene herself was chosen by Jesus to declare the resurrection message to his disciples! Imagine that...a woman preaching the first resurrection message!

The Old Testament prophet known as Jeremiah predicted that women would one day in the future begin to compass men or to go around them in order to fulfill their destiny. That Prophecy is being fulfilled within the pages of this book! Throughout the ages men have often been formidable obstacles, prejudiced obstructions, and demonic hurdles for women in every facet of life. In the area of politics, religion, entertainment, and especially business women are still battling every day for equality and fair pay.

These two authors; Kimberly Jordan and Margaret Parker in this amazing manuscript about the divine feminine have truly captured the essence of the ancient principles taught by the great spiritual avatars like Jesus, Lao Tzu, Buddha, and even Pharaoh Akhenaten of Egypt!

I know these authors; personally. They are holy women. They experientially and academically understand the inner power resident within every person that is always being influenced by our thoughts, words, emotions, imagination, decisions, and actions.

Unlike John the Baptist in the Bible, they have used their faith and the sacred divine resident in them to manifest supernatural deliverance, magical finance, amazing material resources, and physical healing beyond human comprehension!

As you read this book let it become a living epistle for you. Allow the words to penetrate your consciousness and transform your thinking. This is what I know for sure.....If you follow the principles outlined in this book diligently you too, will discover the Infinite One hiding in your own finiteness. I promise.

Pierrette and I consider these two spiritual witnesses as much more than our faithful disciples; they are our personal friends.

May your journey through these pages prove prosperous and life changing!

Enjoy,

D. DeWayne Rudd, Sr. Chief Apostle, CCAC

Acknowledgments

It is with great humility and honor that we take this opportunity to acknowledge and thank those of you who have played such a great and awesome part in the completion of this work. We do not take any contribution, big or small, for granted.

We thank and acknowledge each other, Kimberly Jordan and Margaret Parker, who came together as a melding of spirits to bring this to fruition. Kimberly had a brilliant vision for presenting information to women that can bring them enlightenment as we had received. She so graciously invited me to share in this wonderful journey. I am thankful for this test as it has enabled us to recognize and utilize various gifts and skills that were not being used to their potential.

We wish to thank and acknowledge our Spiritual leader, mentor, and Spiritual father, Chief Apostle D. Dewayne Rudd, Sr., pastor and teacher of Christ Consciousness Awareness Center (CCAC). Chief Apostle's labor of love has been very instrumental in our spiritual growth. He not only shares scriptural insight but presents educational and historical facts that are usually not being taught in a church.

Both, Kimberly and I are very grateful and appreciative of his downloads into our lives. He and other CCAC members will recognize his teachings and maybe some of his quotes. Thank you, Chief Apostle.

We acknowledge *Divine Oneness* for its input and information into this labor of love. The information that we gleaned from them was priceless.

Finally, we want to thank our family and friends. The special people who put up with us and provided what was needed to make the accomplishment worthwhile.

Preface

Divine Woman by Design is a guide. A guide to assist the reader in traveling the journey we present to them into specific, definitive areas of their lives that are broken and hurt; then move into a higher level of consciousness; transferring both their physical and mental well-being on this journey that will inform, heal, and transform.

Every woman should know that God takes precious time developing each and every one uniquely – we all have a unique design that is virtuous and of pure loving energy. Women, we are made wholly in the image of the one true God. There is much entailed in this design process however, and we believe that a woman's inner beauty must be made known to *her* first. The inner beauty of a woman is what gives that woman her character and helps establish who she is and who she will become; and even how she will become. Our society has painted an unrealistic and somewhat deceptive picture of what a woman of power truly is. Society characterizes a woman based on the outside like her accomplishments, her husband, her dress size, her degree, etc. and looks very little within the woman to her heart. A woman's true beauty begins and comes from within; her spiritual make-up. There must be a solid spiritual foundation before the outside structure is formed properly and appears beautiful. God designs a woman's beauty from within --- out! He works on the spirit, her mindset, knowing the outward beauty will be justified by what's projected from her spirit within. God's word says spirit is mind and mind is spirit. Spirit is important in the making of a *Divine Woman by Design*. What did God have in his spirit (in his mind) when making woman? God knows a woman's spirit is reflected in her mindset as it concerns her and life. A woman's spirit is wrapped in her knowing God and having the same mindset God has about her. Some questions to ask yourself would be: How can a woman get to this state or point in her life? How does a woman learn to love herself first and then love others? What mindset should she have? What does God use to design a woman's spirit?

When a woman goes within and reflects her higher self, her eternal self, her real self - - there she will find a Divine Woman by Design.

Introduction

The mindset that we want to project, and ask the reader to contemplate, is to be open minded, flexible, and not afraid of new ideas or new ways of thinking. Take all your preconceived ideas and notions, place them in your mental vault and receive this new consciousness. Like any new thing it is our desire that *Divine Woman by Design* builds on your current way of thinking and living; providing updated and accurate scriptural and historically based information to achieve a new way of thinking and living. It is our belief that new can be good albeit sometimes painful. We also believe that this new way of living and thinking may initiate health and propel you deeper on the special journey of your life. Additionally, we ask that you embrace the science presented and accept the truths as they are referenced in scripture and

the Tao. The Tao is the God within you. It is your inner

Spirit; it is the Way. The Way to living your life abundantly,

prosperously, and in good health. The scriptures are used

as a reference because of its endurance and longevity.

Also, because we believe that it is a roadmap of such for this

journey we call life. More so, we believe that the bible is

truthfully written but not all of it is THE TRUTH!

This information is presented in a simple, understandable

and tangible way that we believe will bring enlightenment,

peace and restoration to the reader and thus, a new

consciousness. We believe that this restoration and new

level of consciousness will affect you to the point of positive

change and the recognition of truth. For we know that the

truth shall set us free. No one can have a full life without

freedom. Freedom to become, freedom to do, freedom to

have, and freedom to experience all that we were created to become, to do, to have, and to experience.

Finally, you will discover specifically who God really is, who you really are in God, and correct the errors and falsehoods that we have been taught and lived. This will be a truth to set you free.

From the Start ...

Divine Woman by Design all started from a study on Queen Esther and how she was anointed, both literally and figuratively, to become Queen and save a nation; her people the Jews. Most of us know the story of how Esther was chosen to be part of the many but ended up becoming the most important one under the King, the Queen. The practices then were to purify virgins before they were presented to the King. This purification period consisted of 12 months including physically cleansing by anointing them with very specific oils. Oils that not only purified physically but also signified specific spiritual cleansing symbolically.

The story goes that Esther was to go before the King (which you did not do unless he sent for you) and make a plea for the Jewish nation. But Esther was no fool, she underwent the purification and received the anointing's that they symbolized. Esther's design after purification we believe is that of a *Divine Woman by Design.* So let us examine the spiritual purification process of Esther and breakdown the symbolism of the oils used to anoint her. A better example for *Divine Woman by Design* we don't believe we could have found.

Esther 2:12 states, *"Now when every maid's turn was come to go in to the king Ahasuerus, after that she had been twelve months, according to the manner of the women (for so were the days of their purifications accomplished, to wit, six months with oil of myrrh, and six months with sweet odours,* (which we research and have broken down) *and with other things for the purifying of the women."* Beginning with the myrrh. Spiritually speaking myrrh represents excellence.

Esther had to have the spirit that God wanted her to have in

order to accomplish what he had for her to do. Anointing her

with myrrh or the spirit of excellence. Esther demonstrated

her excellence through her faith and wisdom. Before Queen

Esther went before the King to make a plea for the Jewish

nation, she called a three day fast with her maidens and

herself. She sought God to see what his thinking was; when

and how things should be handled to defeat the plan of the

enemy Haman (Esther 4:16). She did not go storming out to

the King with her hands on her hips and her head spinning.

Her faith in God lead her to believe that he had appointed

her for this and he could help her bring deliverance to her

people. She sought for godly wisdom and in her getting

godly wisdom she got an understanding also. Additionally,

myrrh in Hebrew means someone who is superior,

exceeding, leaving a plentiful remnant or residue. And the

Greek meaning of myrrh is someone who is superior in rank

of character; they surpass the knowing beyond others and are beyond measure in an abundance, or super eminence; superior, superiority, to be better, have Excellence, to be higher, and supreme – Queen Esther, a *Divine Woman by Design*.

Other sweet fragrances used in Queen Esther's preparation were cinnamon, calamus, cassia, and olive oil. (See Exodus 30:23-26 where these oils are commanded to become holy oils.) So, cinnamon spiritually represents grace. Esther operated in a grace representative of inner beauty that was attractive and receptive and in a spiritual energy that produced favor with God and with man. She was sufficient and proficient in grace which she needed to bring her favor to fulfill her purpose. You see Esther 2:17 states, "... *and she obtained grace and favor in his (King Ahasuerus) sight more than all the virgins.*" And believe me there were plenty of virgins to choose from. Now grace in Hebrew means kindness, well favored, pleasant, and precious. And, the Greek meaning of grace is the divine influence upon the heart and its reflection in life. The grace that Esther had was demonstrated in her character which raised her energy level above the actual circumstance she was faced with causing the heart of the King to eventually soften and change the direction of the Jewish people's lives.

The oil *calamus* represents righteousness (uprightness and right standing). Righteousness the right path for you. Esther was chosen to save a nation and she was chosen because she was willing to do the right thing even though it was not popular with the people but was what the spirit had led her to do. Esther had to go before the King which was a foolish thing if he had not called for her (Esther 4:16b). However her right standing and uprightness put her in a place that was not foolish but of favor providing deliverance for her people.

Finally, olive oil represents the anointing. It is apparent that Esther had something special both in her and on her. Her beauty was inward and outward and it had a dramatic effect on her circumstances, the people she came in contact with and the outcomes that her purpose demanded. Esther humbled herself and did what was right because she had an anointing to do it. Queen Esther used her anointing (power within her) to do mighty exploits and bring deliverance to her people. Now that you have been exposed to the *Divine Woman by Design* in the person of Queen Esther, we can move forward with projecting this image on you. As you can see Esther was the foundation and beginning of our *Divine Woman by Design.*

God is Who (And Why Do We Have to Ask)?

One question that has been heard throughout centuries is, "Who is God and why does he allow this, that and the other?" Well, according to I John 4:8: *God is love*. This does not say that God loves you, which he does. It does not say that God is a loving God although he is. It simply states that God is love and love is an action, a verb with movement. Love is who God is -- NOT what God does! Although it is what He does. We have a tendency to try and make God be what man has decided or deemed him to be but that cannot and will not be. So God is love and love denotes preference meaning that when you love someone or something you prefer that person or thing. And the scriptures expound on who God is by telling us what God does. Let's just be honest, words can be spoken that are truthful or not so truthful but what someone does is a much better and more honest indicator of how they feel about you. "For God so loved the world that he gave…" God gives. So if God is love then love gives. Love gives and does not expect something in return. It has no strings or conditions attached. God loves us without form or measure. There is no depth or height or width or breath or length to measure God's love for us. He draws us to him with his love; his loving kindness which last forever and will not change. For God does not change; he is the same yesterday, today and forever.

As stated above love is an action and I Corinthians 13 speaks volumes of what love is and is not. I.e. love is kind; bears, believes, hopes, and endures all things. It also tells us some of what love is not; love does not seek its own, not easily provoked, and thinks no evil. Love is not fear or envy or jealousy. These are some of the things that love is and is not. Plus God is not a man that he should lie. So we can always expect the truth from God. We did not say from the bible because unfortunately God did not write the bible and we know that is hard to fathom. Let's get this reconciled. If you read the bible from Genesis to Revelations, you will recognize errors, contradictions, and negativity. Throughout the bible you will find murder, human trafficking, genocide, slavery, fear, loathing, hate, and rape, all in the name of God. Then ask yourself are these actions love? The answer is clearly NO. So they cannot be from or of the one true God. This is an error and not correct. The bible was not written by God and we know this because the bible is not perfect. If it had been written by God it would be built upon his nature which is love. But let's face it the bible was written by men and canonized by Constantine, a heathen (take a deep breath and look it up for yourself). The bible was not written by God. It is vitally important to rightly divide the word which allows you to separate error from truth. If it is negative or evil then that is the error we are referring to.

For example, if it is hate, if it is racism, if it is prejudice, etc.,

then that is error we are referencing. If it is love then it is

truth and that is God and that is how you can determine that

something (in the bible) is of God; it will be drenched with

love. So it would stand to reason that the bible then is

truthfully written but not all that is written in the bible is truth.

Selah. So we have to examine the bible and see what truth

is and not just because some man or denomination said it

was truth. We have to examine the scriptures with our Spirit,

discern what is truth and apply that truth using the Spirit that

is within. The God part of man. Because even Jesus said

that we are little gods! And, King David referenced this in

Psalm 82:6 and John 10:34. Look it up and read for

yourself. Selah. Also, ask yourself, "If I am made in the

image of the one true God, I am a measure of who God is,

so that means that I am love just like God is in measure ...

right?" I know, Selah!

God is light also. Light when referenced in the Hebrew

language is energy. In John 5:35 we are told that "He was a

burning and a shining light (energy), and ye were willing for a

season to rejoice in his light (energy)." God is the giver of

what we need, want and desire and from his word he has

given energy and understanding to all. To understand that

light is energy, let's look at electricity. Encyclopedia.com

states that electricity is a form of energy caused by the

presence of electrical charges in all matter. Now just where

do you suppose that all matter originates from? The original

energy or light is God. When God said let there be and then

there was, there had to be something between let there be

and then there was. The answer is ENERGY; pure and

simple. Energy according to Bing is the capacity for vigorous

activity; available power; and an adequate or abundant

amount of such power. (We believe creating the universe

qualifies for those definitions! Don't you?) God's power

generated the energy needed to provide for his creation

ensuring that there was enough of all things at all times in all ways for us to have what we want, need, and desire always.

Also, God is Spirit and Spirit is mind. We know you may have immediately thought of Genesis 1:1 where it says "and the spirit of God moved upon the face of the waters." You probably envisioned a Casper the ghost like entity moving around the earth. Funny, but so not true. But let us examine another scripture for understanding looking at Exodus 35:31: And he hath filled him with the spirit (mind) of God, in wisdom, in understanding, and in knowledge, and in all manner of workmanship; or Deuteronomy 34:9: And Joshua the son of Nun was full of the spirit (mind) of wisdom. We already know that God breathed the breath of life in us at creation and therefore we have his life force spirit in us automatically but like Jesus who grew in wisdom and stature, we have had to learn things about God and learning is done in and with the mind. God gives us so many things to enjoy but 2 Timothy 1:7 tells us that he has not given us a spirit of fear; but of power, love and a sound mind.

An Examination of Scripture

Examining the scriptures has given us some insight into who God is and who God is not. We must now look at who we have been taught God is by our usually "religious" overseers, preachers, ministers and whatever else you call them. One example, is the hell fire and brimstone guys that believe that God would send his very own creation to a pit of continuous destruction; a continuous barbeque if you will. But as referenced earlier, the bible is truthfully written but not all that is in the bible is truth. We have been taught that God operates on fear and that fearing God meant just that; be afraid, be very afraid. However, correct teaching will provide the proper translation of reverence, respect, admire or worship God. Reverence, honor or respect felt or shown, for

God is a more accurate way that we should feel about our Creator in awe of His love and unmatched inward presence. As we shift to correct thinking we get a more accurate definition of who God is. We ask this question so you will recognize the error in how most of us have been taught who God is. And begin to develop and establish our new appreciation of who God really is. As we discussed, God is energy and we are one. So as one, why would we want to bring harm to ourselves? God would not and does not. Unfortunately, religion, which is manmade, introduced these ideas through ignorance and translation error; not to mention control and/or financial gain (which we choose not to explore). Remember, the bible was written by men for a heathen with an ulterior motive named Constantine. (You should probably look Brother Constantine up and how the bible was canonized.) If you ever attended almost any church you were probably taught to fear God for he may get you some day and send you to a burning hell. Taught that only one religion is the true religion. Taught that if you don't confess Jesus as Lord you will go to that burning hell. And I could go on ad nauseam on the things we have been taught about our loving God that are just not in his nature. Therefore they are not true. So we repeat, God is love and love is not any of those things. Man has manipulated, changed and altered the scriptures to fit into their religion. And we all recognize that man is capable of some pretty terrible things. Things that man likes to attribute to God. But God's ways are not our ways.

Additionally, we can tell who God is by the names that we have identified him with. Names from the scriptures that man has given God based on his experience with God. We shall examine these names and provide some general insight to assist you in recognizing them and what they stand for. Also provided are personal insights as to what a specific name has meant to us. You can know the name of someone but not know that someone. So it is with God, we may know his names but do those names mean anything to us; have we experienced what those names mean. That is the only way that the names will become real in your life; when you actually experience what the name means for yourself. You might ask, how we experience the ways of God. Thanks for asking. Some of our experiences have come through the names of God and what those names mean allegorically. (Look up allegory.) Let us examine some of his names.

Jehovah Raah

The chief meaning of Jehovah is derived from the Hebrew word Havah meaning "to be" or "to exist." Raah is derived from Roeh, which means shepherd in Hebrew. A shepherd, one who feeds or leads his flock to pasture. An extended translation of this word is "rea" a "friend" or "companion." This indicates the intimacy God desires between himself and his people. When the two words are combined – Jehovah Raah it can be translated as "The Lord my Friend." And yes, I can truthfully say that the Lord is my friend and also is my shepherd. The attributes that this connotes are burned into my existence. As a friend, he is always near, present and there when needed. I can go deep within myself, where the kingdom of God resides, and have and obtain what I need. As my shepherd he follows a more spiritual path. Leading me to where I need to go and giving me the information I need to make the right choices and decisions in my journey of life.

The old folks used to say "follow your first mind and it won't lead you wrong!" Well my belief is that our first mind, which is being referred to, is our spirit mind. The one that comes from a higher place that resides within us and we can hear sometimes in a still small voice.

Jehovah Rapha

Another experience I had that matches up with one of the names of God in the bible is Jehovah Rapha which means the Lord Who Heals used in Exodus 15:26. Rapha (rapa) means "to restore," or "to heal" or "to make healthful" in Hebrew. When the two words are combined – Jehovah Rapha – it can be translated as "Jehovah Who Heals." Jehovah Rapha is the physician who heals you physically and emotionally. I grew up in a structured home with two parents and a brother. Everything seemed to be going well until one day I witnessed a sad incident and peace was no longer present or visible in the home. As a child I witnessed incidents that were not an expression of love nor peace. My mother was served divorce papers by a Sheriff. I really took my parents' divorce hard. Seeing the discouragement and struggle of my mother and father over a long period of time caused me to internalize my feelings with no out which allowed those same feelings to set up residence in my spirit and soul creating anger, animosity, and remorse. I carried these internal hurtful feelings for years and they became a part of me; so much so until the hurt, pain, and discouragement caused me to become physically ill and emotionally imbalanced. As a result of physical illness and emotional imbalance it became necessary for me to endure the process of two surgeries. Going through this process caused me to seek the God within me for healing and peace. Jesus in Luke 4:23, told us "…physician heal thyself." I learned healing from within and that healing fostered peace. I did not receive physical healing until I went within and communed with my Higher Self – the God in me. I had to discover that my healing was rooted in forgiveness. Forgiveness led to emotional health that began with forgiving myself first. I made myself ill by holding on to other unpleasant experiences during my childhood and the pain of separation and divorce of my parents; fueled by the seeds of animosity and the burden of anger. Therefore, if I made myself ill by holding on, I could in turn make myself healed by letting go. The only way I released the grip of sickness within my body was through love and forgiveness. Love and forgiveness gave me healing in my soul. The healing of my soul, yielded wholeness, so I could regain the balance of my emotions and truly be free.

Jehovah Shammah

Another name of God in the Bible that experienced is Jehovah Shammah – the Lord is there. Shammah is derived from the Hebrew word sham, which can be translated as "there." Jehovah Shammah is a symbolic name for the earthly Jerusalem. The name indicates that God has not abandoned Jerusalem, leaving it in ruins, but that there will be a restoration. Jehovah Shammah was revealed to me on an icy street in Little Rock, Arkansas on a wintry December day. I was driving my son to the airport to fly to spend

Christmas with his father in St. Louis. The weather had

taken a turn for the worse as soon as we left the house, as it

is prone to do in Little Rock at the drop of a hat, so I

determined that my son would not miss his opportunity to

have Christmas with his father. We started out slowly in our

winding road neighborhood. I was cautious to keep an eye

out for other drivers. As we approached a street going down

an incline I noticed a car coming up on us at an unsafe

speed for the icy and snowy conditions. My son sensed my

concern and turned to see what was happening. He quickly

said, "That car is going too fast!" So I tapped my brakes to

indicate that we were slowing down but to no avail. I tapped

them again as we got further down the inclined street; again

to no avail. I began to brake so that I could control the

speed of my dissent and my car began to swerve. At the

exact same time the car behind me started to swerve. We

are swerving in tandem! So my son and I both shouted "God

– No!" At that point I don't have any recollection of stopping the car. But ... both cars stopped side by side at a 90° angle to the curb so close that the driver of the other car could not open his door to get out but we are not touching. We both get out and he is an older gentleman who immediately says to me that he does not know how his car stopped! But my son immediately says, "because God is here!" Jehovah Shammah. A man appears jogging from out of nowhere and helps us get our cars separated and I get my son to the airport in time. He was there whether you believe it or not.

Jehovah Mekoddishkem

Here is another name of God that has been experienced by us. Jehovah Mekoddishkem - The Lord Who Sanctifies You - is first used in Exodus 31:13. Mekoddishkem derives from the Hebrew word qadash meaning "sanctify," "holy," or "dedicate." Sanctification is the separation of an object or person to the dedication of the Holy. When the two words are combined - Jehovah Mekoddishkem - it can be translated as "The Lord who sets you apart." I am prone to believe that if we cultivate our spirit and our spiritual journey we will become set apart. Not necessarily different but yes different and on another level. That other level does not mean better level but different. I believe that knowing and believing in someone or something that is greater than you does set you apart and will make life different and better. Also, sanctification comes when you remove yourself from the space of others who do not vibrate on your level. There are times when you say, "I am just not feeling you," or you may think I do not like the 'vibe' I am getting from this person. As we journey in life we find that people will stay in our lives for only a period of time. Once that time has elapsed they either leave our space or we leave their space. I personally have experienced three friends moving from my immediate vibrational space who had been in my life for a number of years. I noticed that we had grown apart

spiritually and our spiritual places were on different levels. I

think of this as a temple experience described in the bible

where it talks about the outer court, the inner courts, and the

Holy of Holies. The outer court is where associates dwell,

like Facebook friends and Twitter friends; the inner court is

where family members and "really close friends" dwell; and

the Holy of Holies is you, your spouse or significant other.

These particular friends moved from my inner court to the

outer court. They are no longer in my immediate vibrational

space and I am good with that.

Jehovah Jireh

And another! Jehovah Jireh - The Lord Will Provide. It is

used in the Old Testament only once in Genesis 22:14

Jehovah Jireh is a symbolic name given to Mount Moriah by

Abraham to memorialize the intercession of God in the

sacrifice of Isaac by providing a substitute for the imminent sacrifice of his son. There have been many experiences for me with Jehovah Jireh literally. For example, when I was a single mother just moving into a new home with my youngest son. My two other children had grown and gone. It took every cent I had to move and establish our home. So I am sitting in bed one evening and I am about to have the pity party of a lifetime with no money for food, school, clothes, etc. So I began to cry out to God. Tears and snot and more tears and more snot. I pulled out my bible and said show me what I need to know or don't ever talk to me again. My bible opens to Genesis 22:14 and I read the story of Abraham and Isaac on Mount Moriah. Now I am confused and wondering what sacrificing a son has to do with my lack, shortage and insufficiency. Surely I will not have to sacrifice my son! Had God lost his mind, was it me or what the heck! At that point I clearly heard as I took care of Isaac I will take care of you. But I did not see any taking care of going on. I cried myself to sleep that night. When I woke up my Spirit told me to check my bank account and as usual I argued why. Neither believing nor knowing that what I had asked for was trying to be revealed to me. But my Spirit was quite incessant so I called the bank and I had a balance of $2,214 (Genesis 22:14) dollars in my account which consisted of less than $25 the night before at the pity party. So I am intimately and deeply acquainted with Jehovah Jireh.

Jehovah Shalom

The last name that we want to reference is Jehovah Shalom - The Lord is Peace. In the Old Testament Jehovah Shalom only occurs once in Judges 6:24. Shalom is a derivative of shalem (which means "be complete" or "sound" shalom is translated as "peace" or "absence from strife.") Jehovah-Shalom is the name of an altar built by Gideon in Ophrah. I have experienced being in a place of having no peace. I got married at age 32 and lived in this marriage for 10 years

where I was actually single and lonely, although I had a

"piece of paper" showing that I was married; I experienced

rejection that put me in a mindset that maybe something was

wrong with me. I questioned my own worth-my very own

value. After my divorce, the God within me spoke "treat

yourself like royalty. Live by loving you and love will be

returned unto thee." I did as instructed and have seen

positive results. I have learned loving the one I see in the

mirror every day is the beginning of loving others. Loving

yourself is vital to staying ALIVE and being a blessing.

Appreciating me as the precious creation and embracing all

of me is love. Understanding myself – my strengths – my

weaknesses, the good, and my areas that are still under

construction is vital for me completing this journey

successfully. Trying to love someone else without first loving

and learning the one you see in the mirror daily creates a

void in you. It invites negative energy (people who do not

mean you any good) into your space. Negative energy welcomes rejection, abuse (physical, mental, and emotional), low self-esteem, and self-pity. In addition the lack of peace in this relationship hindered my prosperity. After divorcing and learning to love me, peace has been re-established in my life and I have experienced restoration. *I Am* peace, experiencing prosperity in my life!

Practically speaking, we have tried to guide and give you insight and provide life experience into what God and his names can mean and do. If you look hard enough and meditate on these names, I bet you will be able to achieve the same.

Practically Speaking

Okay, as a *Divine Woman by Design*, to this point we have examined who God is and our divine oneness. Consequently we have made a conscious concerted documented effort to highlight and correct specific errors that have been jammed down our throats by religion. We have tried to provide alternative options to a spiritually connected way of life as opposed to the man-made religious dogma permeating the world today. This alternative spiritual way of life was not an easy path to find and/or continue to follow. Because how can you learn without a teacher and how can you take a path that you don't know even exists. Our path to becoming a *Divine Woman by Design* is still being traveled and we suspect will stay traveled until we reach our end.

This journey of spiritual awakening, mental and physical well-being, and enlightenment has many levels and varying degrees of information, experience, knowledge and even healing for our soul and body. Some of this trip I was aware of and some of it I did not become aware of until I was able to see it in others and assist them in coming out of it. That is assuredly how it works, you learn to help yourself by helping others.

Fortunately or unfortunately, my journey had a very religious foundation in the African Methodist Episcopal Zion (AME Zion) Church (and some Missionary Baptist) overseen by my Grandmother who reigned supreme over our household. She was Mudea before Tyler Perry as I suspect lots of others were also. She was strict, straightforward, honest, informative, and what I really believed, all knowing. But, most of all, she was loving as I only learned much later in life. Her name is on the "cornerstone" of our family church.

Divine Woman by Design

You see we attended church like we did school or work,

religiously. If we did not go to church, then we did not go

anywhere else. We attended Sunday school, 11 am service,

the 3 pm program, and the 6 pm BTU service. Let's not

forget Wednesday night prayer service also. At each one of

these events AME Zion Church doctrine was up close and

personal drilling into our consciousness the belief that "God"

was going to get me. I was a sinner hell bound that only the

AME Zion church could save. However, for me, I could

never reconcile that if God was love, why would His love

lead to a barbeque for me. That confusion led me to leave

organized religion and as a result I became aware of my

inner self. (The self I now know is my God-self from the

breath of life imparted into me). The self that could do

anything! There was no name for it and I certainly did not

attribute it to a higher power but I was allowed to recognize

that if I said things and concentrated on those things, then

they would come true. Therefore, I became self-aware and

went on a journey far from AME Zion man-made religion as one could possibly go; and I am very thankful for that particular part of the journey.

Being away from organized religious had negative societal consequences that were not very pleasant. If you did not attend the local church, plus believed that you could accomplish and do anything, then something was very wrong with you. You were labeled an egotistical hedonistic sinner that was borderline narcissistic and probably in need of medication and/or deliverance. But I persevered and thrived to some degree. Obtaining and maintaining what I did not really recognize as a relationship with my inner self which I now know to be my God self. If it felt right to me then I did it and mostly with high levels of success. But there was always that foundation of religion in the back of my mind "religiously" pulling on my conscious. Questioning what was wrong with me that I had strayed from what I had been taught all my life.

Subsequently, a conflict ensued in my inner being that resulted in my abandonment of religious and spiritual thinking and doing. I allowed outside influences like men, sex, drugs and a myriad of other things to take me away. It did not feel good anymore, so I had to have something to take its place. Men were a challenge and an easy conquest back then; which was more than 40 years and 50 lbs ago. I was thin, cute and very confident. Plus, at the time I lived in Los Angeles, California where money was king and anything goes. Well I went with just that, anything. Numbing my senses to reality and building a deep black hole that would take years to get out of. Years of letting someone else dictate who and what I was and what I would do. Years of letting go of what I had been brought up to think and do. Years of struggle with who I thought I was and who society said I was. It was a war of epic proportions with numerous battles; some I won and some I lost. Never realizing that I was in this war only knowing that something was not right in my world and I had to change it or it would not change. So here is what happened.

I moved back home and decided that I needed to discover myself again. The self that I loved and that loved me back. The self that was confident. The inner self that had given me so much positive in the past but I had abandoned for outside influences. Remember I was in a black hole. I had lots of climbing to do. Fortunately, for me I was introduced to a church. A church where religion was almost a bad word. Self was the most important thing taught from the scriptures and taught with such practicality that it could be used in everyday life to make it better. A self that was one with the creator and dwelled inside of me. It took me a long time but we became friends. We became BFFs. We became one. And, this is my desire for you! Become one

with your creator. Becoming one with your creator, you find

your divinity – *Divine Woman by Design*. There is no

separation in oneness – only unconditional love.

Oneness with the Divine

As a "Divine Woman by Design" let's examine and enter into who we really are. In John 10:34, Jesus states, "I and my Father (God) are one." God is love and God is the eternal nature of love. Love is who God is. God (love) gives. If love is who God is; how is it that God can endorse any negative activity? God (Love) allows all beliefs we have because love knows that truth will ultimately be discovered by those who seek it. Love expects all things to conclude in love. Love hopes for the best in all things. Love endures all without ever refraining from Love. Love cannot fail to receive what love wants. God gave us his only begotten son that he might live through him. Love is right there; it gives unconditionally and expects nothing in return. Love does not want what it does not have to give. You see Paul the

Apostle gives us a basic description of love and therefore of

God in I Corinthians 13:4-8. Love is eternal patience. Love

never gives up or "throw in the towel." Love has more

concern for others than for itself. Love is eternal kindness

and God draws us with his loving kindness. Love is never

jealous or boastful. Love is not arrogant, strutting itself to be

seen by others. Love does not have a "me, myself and I"

(selfish) attitude. Love never seeks its own way, wishes evil

upon others and love does not fly off the handle. Love does

not reject what it does not understand. Love embraces the

challenge and seeks the lesson to establish a successful

experience. Love never speaks wrong of others. Love is

never provoked to do anything harmful to another. Love

never acts inappropriately with malicious intent. Love is

sensitive enough to recognize that hurting people hurt

people. Love does not hurt! Love does not have space for

evil consciousness. And, love does not keep score or tally of other people's mistakes. Love has a distinct image.

He made us in His image, so we are one, God and I; you and God; you and me. We are one and, within a divine oneness, because that is part of our design. A design predicated on a Universal Spiritual Law called the *Law of Divine Oneness.* The Law of Divine Oneness gives us a fundamental understanding that we are all connected to each other, and that we are all connected to the same Divine God. As spiritual light filling a human body we exist in both a physical and spiritual world co-existing here on earth physically and spiritually through our oneness with the Divine. Truthfully, we have found numerous ways to separate ourselves from each other. However, the Universal Spiritual Law of Oneness makes us aware and conscious that we are one. Collectively, we are a group of spiritual beings having a human experience. The intent is that as we learn and mature we grow into the knowledge we need to

accept and nurture our divine oneness. Although each of us

as individuals has our own path and direction, we still come

from the same source, the One.

When you look around at our societies, our world, our nation,

our states, our cities, our neighborhoods, and even our

homes, these realities reinforce our separateness. We may

not look alike. We may have different languages, different

ideas, different morals, different spiritual teachings and

paths. But ... the Law of Divine Oneness makes us

consciously aware and spiritually remember that we are a

family collective of humans, united in our Oneness and

spiritually supported equally by the One.

The purpose of the Law of Divine Oneness is to bring

together our conscious minds and to open our hearts to

compassion for one another, joy in everything we do,

support for one another and from the One, gratitude for each and everything, and appreciation of one another as we walk our separate paths. This Law works to return us to the place of love (where we originated), acceptance of our Oneness, and enjoyment that comes from being a part of Oneness. From a practical standpoint let us examine some examples of oneness in our real world. This should and will assist you in visualizing our Divine Oneness.

This universal spiritual law is conscious awareness that although we have found many ways to separate ourselves as individuals with defining labels, we are all energetically One. We each possess sovereign individual power from the same Source and we choose to use it in different ways and at different times in our soul's growth. Collectively, we are a group of spiritual beings who are having a human experience with the intention of developing more fully in whatever ways our soul needs to grow. This is where physical individuation takes form – yet the Source energy is the same.

Unfortunately, life on earth gives us the illusion that we are separate from each other and most of all separate from God. We have been taught and darn near brainwashed into believing that God is in some heaven that is far, far away. We have been taught that God is not love but some schizophrenic being like us that wants to judge, condemn and then send us straight to hell without passing go and not collecting $200. How many times have you heard that God is going to get you? It starts early. Do as your religion says or the schizo God will get ya! No heaven for you! No streets paved with gold. You know the story! So this type of indoctrination leads to walls of defense and barriers to love and oneness. But these constructs of religion can be brought down when we are consciously aware of our Divine Oneness. When you understand the Spiritual Law of Divine

Oneness, you accept your own Divine Oneness – *Divine Woman by Design*. As we learned the inaccurate, incorrect, and hurtful dogmas of religion, now we must change the mind, attitude and actions of the only person we have any and total control over; ourselves. Let it go and learn to accept the change that Divine Oneness creates. Oneness with everyone and everything. How can we, for in all intents and purposes, be anything or anyone other than what created us. Humans create humans, animals create animals, and plants create plants; so God created gods or little creators. Practically speaking, let us examine some truths that may rev up your believing in our Divine Oneness. Beginning with your believing that we and God are one. For example, Genesis tells us that the breath of life was breathed into us and we became living beings. Do you have to tell yourself to breath? To make your heart beat, whether awake or sleep? Do you alert your muscles to move so you can function and perform various tasks? Do you tell your eyes to blink and clean themselves? Do you tell your brain

to function? Do you think and/or believe that you are so

special that YOU make all these things happen? What on

earth, cause we are on earth, allows and causes you to

move and breath and have your being? The very one and

the same thing that when it exits your earthly body will cause

it to cease to exist, your Oneness with the creator.

Divineness in a human body. *Divine Woman by Design.*

God is Love

So now that you are contemplating your Divine Oneness, you can also begin to accept that because God is love as the scripture (I John 4:8) tells you, then he created us as love also. This God of love resides in us. Luke 17:21 states the kingdom of God is within us. God is not an outside entity, perched on a throne in a city not made by hands that sits at the end of the streets paved with gold! He is not something that is separate and distinct from us. After all if God blew himself into our earthly bodies, then God is everywhere we are because he is in us. We are who created us.

We are one with God, which is such awesome greatness, that we must learn to tap into and use to live, the Oneness life. The Oneness life of wholeness nothing missing, nothing broken and nothing lacking. God is the infinite intelligence within us at the highest level of intellect which directs us to love, peace, spirituality, and awakened consciousness that creates and exists in love. This enlightened intelligent spirit within knows all, since it is the express application of not only common sense, but inner knowledge confirming our need to better understand who we are. We are one with our Father. All of us! When we look at other people and other creations, we are looking at God. God, who breathed himself into all of our multiple unique disguises with unique structures of diversity. These diverse structures assist us in learning, teaching, and guidance. You see God wanted to experience many different experiences so he created Asian, African, Japanese, Jewish, Muslim, and many other nationalities and cultures. All these differences allow us so much to appreciate. He lives his creation! That's right! We are being lived – and probably never realized it. WOW!

Divine Woman by Design

Take a Selah and think about that. We are many of the One

true God! The God who is a creative spiritual loving energy

that exists in all, through all, and around all. Omnipresent!

Selah again.

We believe that divine oneness is the connection with our

creator and all other creation. There is a perfect unity

between all of us. The color, the nationality, the creed, the

origin does not matter! We are one regardless of our races,

our color, what language we speak, where we were born,

etc. God purposed diversity therefore diversity is so. We

should embrace one another's differences, so we may learn

from one another.

You see divine Oneness is love for yourself and love for all

creation. We love from within, where God is located. Love

is who created us. God is Love. He made us in his image.

"I and my Father are one." John 10:34. Therefore, be who

you really are and that is Love. Love assists someone no matter what color they are. Love feeds a person or an animal who is hungry. Love gives a hug to a hurting child or adult regardless. Love tells someone the truth. Love heals a broken heart. LOVE DOES NOT HURT! Love expresses the divinity in everyone – all creation. Divine oneness is the connection between all creations that is tied to the Source which created it. We are one mind, one spirit, one body created for the purpose to love. Love is the cohesive force that keeps us whole and connected to the true source and that is the Creator.

Here is what divine Oneness looks like in the real world according to Molly McCord and Conscious Cool Chic. The ocean: The Divine Oneness of oceans is that we are all surrounded by water, composed of water and rely on water for basic survival. The oceans are a symbol of all that we value and cherish on the planet, a precious resource for every physical being. However, looking at the 2010 BP oil spill we see an excellent example of how something happening in one part of the ocean can travel to multiple other destinations and affect millions of people around the world. Treating our oceans and all water resources with respect is a reflection of the law of Divine Oneness. What happened in one location affected all locations. As it is with us what affect one affects us all. So like the Divine Oneness of our oceans, we all are a part of the One. If I contaminate and disrespect you, I am contaminating and disrespecting all; including myself. So let us treat each other with respect and love as we live in this ocean called life. Divine Oneness.

Asked and Answered

As noted earlier, we are one with our Father. We are made in his image and his likeness. By now we should be able to concede that our bodies and our spirits are separate and distinct; with our bodies, at their end, returning to where it originated, earth; and our spirits returning to where it originated, God. So if we originated from God and God is love, then I will hypothesize that what God had in his mind when he made us as *Divine Women by Design*, was a human being of love; to love. Remember that love is a verb showing action; it gives. So if man came first then I believe that God wanted man and himself to have an object to give to and to love. He wanted an object to bestow his changing love on. An object that would return that love thus allowing God to receive that which he gives. SELAH!

Practically speaking, what good would it do and what purpose would it serve to have the wonderful gift of love and not be able to share it, receive it, and/or experience it. Therefore, we believe that God made woman to receive, share and experience. To receive love, share wisdom and experience all that he has made available; instilling in the woman the God love that gives. So that first, a woman is divine in that she is one with the creator and originated from the creator and therefore is a creator. He designed this divine being to receive and give love. Because God is not a man he is not going to manifest in the earth as we have been led and taught to believe. God manifests through his creations. So as his creations in the earth women carry love and nurture. Loving and nurturing themselves first, their families, their friends, their environments, etc.

Divine Woman by Design

The D*ivine Woman by Design*, and even society, sees her like this as the who, who receives and then produces. A divine woman as with any precious object should be loved, protected and taken care of; placed in the highest esteem. Allowed to be as she was created to be; a *Divine Woman by Design.*

If we are *Divine Women by Design* created and nurtured by our Father then why are we not living that divine status? First, we would offer that we are not really born into that environment. We are not brought up and taught that we are designed in the image and likeness of our Father and we are not loved and nurtured as he designed us to be. Thus we have to first become aware of the need for love and nurturing, obtain that love and nurturing and then begin to practice love and nurturing. We say practice it because we believe that we do not reach mastery of divineness but experience various levels though our understandings and lives. Even when we practice love and nurturing practically speaking, we do not normally love and nurture ourselves. We may be taught and trained by our society that we are to be the lovers and nurturers of others specifically our husbands/wives, children, etc. However, nowhere in that learning is there a mention of loving and nurturing one's self.

So, we go about our lives caught in a vicious circle of trying to do something that we are ill equipped and unlearned in doing. And, we perpetrate that circle and cycle through our families, friends and others. At some point we may have an epiphany and become self-aware. Aware that we are not just a wife, not just a mother, or not just Mrs. So in So. We become aware that we are made in the image and likeness of the one true God and that that one true God is love. Something that can overcome all. We then step into that awareness with a fervor that leaves no room for lack, shortage or insufficiency. We step into an awareness that we are one with our creator and that we are thus creators

able to do exceedingly abundantly above what we could ask

or think. This self-awareness brims from inside out and

changes you, your life and the people around you; *Divine*

Woman by Design.

Recognizing the Divine Feminine

Now that we are beyond foundational and into the heart of

the matter, let us delve into answering the questions

presented at the beginning of this book. *What did God have*

in his spirit (in his mind) when making woman? First what a

woman thinks of herself is paramount. It begins with

understanding the basics as woman is created in the image

and likeness of her creator, God. Since the creation is in

God's image, she is spirit, she is mind; she is consciousness

as learned in earlier chapters. Christ is the mind or

consciousness of God, not the last name of Jesus; but that is another topic altogether. So woman is the pure essence of God's consciousness. God is love, God is light, and God is spirit. Therefore, God's consciousness is love, spirit, and light. Let us look at these individually.

Love

***Love* is preference**. Who or what is choice. God chose you. We can take this a step further by recognizing Psalm 34:10 when it states, "Ye are Gods", and so if we are who created us in his image, we are little gods, creators/love. God had in his mind love when he made woman. Woman is naturally love because love is giving. Love is caring, love is nurturing, love is patient, and love is kind and gentle. Woman in spirit is what God is and that is her divine creation.

Spirit

Spirit **is the invisible** that is so prevalent when it is revealed through love. Spirit is all knowing, perfect in all its beautiful forms. Spirit is quiet but knows perfect timing when rising to take action. That is woman, Woman is wise. Woman is the divine feminine wisdom of God. Woman is divinely made in wisdom of God's mind – his consciousness. Woman can conceive and process multiple things simultaneously.

Light

Light **is knowledge**, light shines and reveals the path to the kingdom of God that is with us. Light illuminates the purpose of existing. Light promotes evolution of the soul. We come to this school called earth to evolve. Light is the way to staying connected to the divine energy of the Most High. God had evolution in mind when he created woman.

Divine Woman by Design

Woman is the way for all mankind to come into awareness of spirit and truth.

Woman is the divine feminine, the energy of light, love, and spirit; which are all God himself formed in feminine energy. This divine Feminine is the medium and substance of creation. This truth is fundamental and profound, every woman knows this within. Flowing from the substance of her very being life occurs. Woman can conceive and produce. She is a great participant in bringing a soul into the earth. A woman giving birth is an expression of love.

In child bearing a woman gives all she is to bring forth creation. Society's ideas and their stereotypes have diminished the entire connection of woman and the loving creation God has designed for her to be.

When we think we are separate from who created us we have lost the reality of who we really are. We ultimately disconnect ourselves from the Divine love, which says we are spirit and we are eternal. You are the creation of God himself and his creation is all love – nothing but love.

Achieving Wisdom

How can a woman get to this state or point in her life?

A woman can reach this state by identifying the wisdom within herself. This wisdom is knowing and accepting that there is no separation between her and her creator. The woman, spiritually speaking, is subconscious. It is feminine energy which is designed to receive. She is receptive to truth that is provided to her by love. The truth is she is divinely made by the god in her for a special and unique purpose. The god within lives purposely through her. She receives the love she needs to be a nurturing being; the peace to accept the silence of Spirit speaking within her; the strength through God's faithfulness; the lessons she embrace by way of being meek; the goodness she sows to herself and in the lives of others; the gentleness she uses when addressing sensitive life situations; the patience she has to stimulate maturity and having balance between the natural and the spiritual. Woman is complex, yet simplistic at dispensing wisdom to evoke growth.

Her complexity allows her to handle multiple things at one time without the results being diluted or lose their integrity. She always understands the true meaning of life invitations. She has comprehension of what life invites her to learn or to teach. Woman also uses the wholeness within her. This wholeness comes from her knowing and understanding the oneness of divine feminine energy and divine masculine energy. There is a unity between feminine (receiving energy) and masculine (providing energy). Feminine energy is spirit. Spirit is sub-consciousness. Masculine energy is natural. This natural energy is consciousness. There is a perfection that exist when both feminine and masculine are balanced. The divine feminine of a woman involves her knowing and understanding what she feels.

It is her instinctual wisdom. A woman knows the connection between these two energies; just as she spiritually and naturally knows how to nourish her children. Until now this knowing has not been the ultimate light for masculine consciousness. The frustration a woman feels is not knowing how to use these two energies together. When these energies are used together it allows the light of the feminine and the darkness of masculine to operate as One creating an inner balance, which allows the infinite intelligence of Spirit to be exhibited. When combining feminine and masculine we understand the pieces that make up the whole. The parts are the events or occurrences that ignite the lessons we come to learn in this realm called earth. The whole is knowing we are complete and one with the energy of the Divine Source. The Divine Source within us designated by our creator. Woman is a powerful and uniquely made being, designed to be Divine.

How does a woman learn to love herself first and then love others? To answer this question, we must remember what love is, what love is not, and what love does. According to 1 Corinthians 13:4-8, Love is patient, love is kind, love is not jealous, love does not boast, love is not puffed (up) arrogant. Love never does anything against the standard or the nature of Love. Love does not demand its own way. Love cannot be persuaded or provoked to do evil. Love does not think evil. Love never rejoices at evil. Love rejoices when truth prevails. Love does not change. Loves' yes is yes and No is No. Loves' promises are yes and Amen (it shall be so). Love believes all things. Love expects all things. Love endures everything without departing from the very thing it is. Love cannot fail.

Keeping this in mind and holding on to the knowledge and understanding that we have; love is the true nature of God. Secondly, let's look at our love for God (our creator). Scripture states in Deuteronomy 6:5 we shall love the Lord thy God with all thine heart, and with all thy soul, and with all our might. If we are who created us then we are made into the image and likeness of our God. We are a god. In John 10:34, Jesus answered the Jews, "Is it not written in your law. I said ye are gods?" We are small gods (creators). According to scripture in Deuteronomy 10:12 we are to fear (meaning reverence) God walk in all his ways, love him, serve him with all thy heart and with all thy soul.

Read this next paragraph as if you are speaking to yourself in the mirror:

If God is love, I am made in his image, I am a small g o d, that means I am who he is, LOVE. Therefore I must reverence the God in me, because I am who he is. I shall live his ways, loving him is first loving me. Falling in love with me! Serving him is serving me with all my mind, will, and emotions. I have to love me – all the way – give myself the best first! We must love ourselves first by doing the things we enjoy doing for ourselves. This could be something as mundane as getting a manicure every week, a pedicure monthly, a body massage every one or two months, enjoying a hobby on a consistent basis, enjoying a cup of tea or coffee while listening to your inner voice. Going fishing or spending time in nature enjoying the beauty that surrounds you. Loving you is exiting toxic relationships. These relationships involve being connected with someone who drains your energy or being connected with someone who physically, emotionally, and/or mentally abuses you! These individuals take-take-take, but never offer anything. Loving you is making sure you keep positive people in your space. These people edify you, and you do likewise for them. These people support your dreams and motivate you to be your BEST! Their purpose is to love you unconditionally and you do the same for them. When you love you, you love God, because ultimately you and God are one. Even Jesus acknowledged this truth, by saying, "…my Father and I are one."

Thirdly, after showing yourself love, you then have what's needed to love other people. You have the strength, the knowledge, the wisdom to love and to give whole heartedly. Matthew 19:19 says, "Thou shalt love thy neighbor as thyself." We ought to love others as ourselves. As you do not "half-step" with handling yourself, do not love or give sparingly to others. For what you do for or to another person; you do unto yourself; because you are that other person and that person is you. We are all one. Jesus, said what you do to the least of them, you do unto me. We are all connected. We are one! "How good and how pleasant it is for brethren to dwell together in unity." Psalm 133:1

Mindset

What mindset should she have? Dealing with the mindset of *Divine Woman by Design* starts with who that woman is and we hope we have established that she is the same as her creator, God. God is love so therefore a *Divine Woman by Design* is love. Her mindset must be rooted and grounded in that concept of love. Nothing that she does nor anything that she says and all that oozes from her must be love.

Without mind we are nothing, nothing but a spirit that has been let loose on the world without direction or purpose. The things that we are taught from birth assist in developing our mindset along with our environment, people we come in contact with and the things that we ultimately decide to do.

Our minds have to be trained in the ways of the *divine* or they will be out of balance with what and who we have been created to be and do. Unfortunately, most of our mind training is not in line with the One True God; the God of love, so ultimately we believe we have phases. The first phase is pure when we are born. The second phase we believe is when we become innately aware of right and wrong. The third phase we believe is when people, places, and things influence our mind set. And finally we believe there is the "I know better, but we have to make a decision phase." There is no right or wrong just what I believe has an impact on our mindset.

But ... there is a spirit in man. And ... if we can connect with that spirit it can determine your mindset and allow you to be and do what you are created to be and do.

What does God use to design a woman's spirit?

Divine Woman by Design

Let's just say that an apple does not fall far from the tree!

We are made in the image and likeness of the Divine creator

therefore we can only be like the Divine Creator. God uses

what he is – LOVE. Love is what make a woman or any

living being. He created woman to receive love. Woman is

the Receiver. She is divinely designed through purity of

love. Love encompasses everything. This everything we

are referring to is wisdom, peace, love, gentleness, joy, faith,

meekness, and balance. Woman is designed to execute her

existence with the combinations of love and faith; love and

peace; love and wisdom, love and knowledge. Woman is

designed to handle multiple things simultaneously leaving

nothing insufficient. Knowledge is her strength to help

others while maintaining her dignity and purpose. Women

are created as the divine feminine that expresses the infinite

intelligence that is within her. Woman is the feminine energy

that is receptive to spirit direction and guidance. Woman

can lead as well as follow without hindering her connection with the Divine.

Our spirits are love and pure energy wrapped in a human container. That container houses peace, joy, wholeness, kindness, patience and all the fruits of the spirit. It is a spirit that is strong and yet tender. It is a spirit of many parts yet whole. It is an intelligent spirit yet always learning. It is a spirit of all that encompasses being human but yet divine.

As a spirit being experiencing a human existence, we all came from the One True God. He is our Father and the giver of life. Therefore, he had to design us in His image using His spirit and likeness as an example. An example in its pure state of divine energy. Energy that does not have an agenda but denotes love, peace, joy and happiness. One with the Father. And, as with all designs, we started with a thought. The great creator wanted to experience being human. Thinking how to place his energy spirit in us. We believe the creator went inside. Sitting on that imaginary throne on the streets paved with gold and drew from all that is the best of him. Drawing from his love, patience, and nurturing, kind energy self.

All that we ever need is inside of us wrapped up in that spirit that part of God that he placed in us, so we could be just like him. The definition of design is to prepare the preliminary sketch or the plans for a work to be executed; to plan and fashion artistically or skillfully; and to assign in thought or intention; purpose. We want to break that definition down and show what God used to design a woman's spirit. First God prepares his preliminary sketch. That sketch comes from the thoughts in his mind that these will be my children, so they should look just like me in my image and likeness. Then our definition say to prepare the plans for a work to be executed. Women are to work at being divine women by design. Placed in us is an energy that will allow us to do exceedingly abundantly above all that we could ask or think. We are to work at being the best image and likeness of the creator that we can be. Next our definition states to plan and fashion artistically or skillfully. We believe that this requires some action on our part at this juncture.

Let's take a look in the mirror.

Look at the skillfully designed work of art you are. Look at yourself from head to toe and see that there is no one like you. We may be all female, but no other female is you.

Finally, our definition says to assign in thought or intention – purpose. God used thought, intention and purpose in his design for our spirit. The thought that we could be his presence in the earth (because you should know that nobody is coming to fix it for you); the intention to place a spirit in you that can handle any situation that it encounters and lastly, our divine purpose in the earth which is distinct and specific for each and every one of us.

Conclusion

The conclusion of the whole matter boils down to one word

we believe – love. We all can spout "For God so loved the

world…" or "love is the answer" but do we really know what

that means – love that is. Many times we have all heard or

even said to ourselves I love the Lord or I love God. But ask

yourself how many times have you told yourself or heard

someone tell themselves I love me. I love me some me.

Probably not many times or not all.

Love is defined by Webster online as warm attachment,

enthusiasm, or devotion and we would agree. But we seem

to reserve this just for others. It seems to me that you could

probably name several if not more people that you have a

warm attachment to, enthusiasm for or devotion to without hesitating. However, let me ask you a question: Why don't you love you more? When was the last time you felt a warm attachment for yourself? Feeling like arms were wrapped around you in a heated blanket leaving you with *that* feeling. When was the last time you felt enthusiasm for who you are? Happy and elated that you are you without spot, wrinkle or blemish; whole. When was the last time you did something out of devotion to yourself? Just did it because it was something nice for you and you would enjoy it? Now if you are honest, as we would hope you to be, it may have been a while in all three instances. But it is in you because you were created with that God love and it can accomplish anything. The conclusion of the whole matter is that we are *Divine Women of Design*. A design that emanated from the creator that is pure and undefiled.

Divine Woman by Design

How can you love someone you cannot see, but cannot love the one you see as a reflection in the mirror every day? How can you say you love someone you cannot see, but you cannot love the people who are in your space who you do see? Many times we tend to say things because it sounds good, but it means nothing. Real true love starts with you. It begins with loving yourself. It begins with loving you just the way your creator made you. You are perfect. SELAH! You are good just the way you are. If you try to change to fit others profile of what they think you should be, you fall into emulation. Emulation is dangerous because you are not true to yourself and no one else. When you really are being you – being yourself there will be someone who does not like you.

Be aware if everyone speaks fondly of you and do not feel bad when others do not like you. If these people were honest they will understand the oneness of all. We are all one – we are the many in the one source. There is a story I would like to tell you about myself concerning the importance of loving you and never loosing that love.

When I was married I would allow myself to go without.... go without loving me. During the course of the marriage, it became all about him. If he had a speaking engagement I was present and supportive. If he was working on a project and needed assistance I was there for him and he did not have to ask me to be there! However, when it came to me. Things were different, if I had a speaking engagement or a project I was working on he was not there and background support was minimal. The sad part is, his actions became okay because I handled it so passively. I was passive to the point I became completely drained and my self- worth totally diminished. When I realized I was giving and not receiving, I made an exit from the relationship through divorce.

What happened? What was the root of the problem in our relationship? I lost who I was...the love for me was thrown on the back burner eventually not even being a priority. When I lost who I was, my husband's level of respect became little to none for me. I drew that to myself.

You cannot expect others to love you and you do not love you. Love starts with you loving you. Never lose the love for you no matter whom you are connected with. Pay attention to yourself. Don't allow issues to become a part of your life without resolution. Love yourself enough to handle your business. Handle it in a way that is mutually beneficial to all involved. Handle your business in love.

What we know for sure is loving you is loving what the creator made you. He made us so perfect. We are divinely made in his image, which is completely whole (lacking nothing)! That is the divine feminine that can never be lost because when it is lost or hindered the connection with divine you is broken causing the spiritual fruit development (love, peace, faith, joy, goodness, meekness, patience, and temperance) to be hindered.

What I know for sure is my ex-husband was invited into my life by me. He was my Governor and my tutor. I signed up for class and had to learn to not stop loving me and do not loose who I am no matter what or who is in connection with me! I appreciate the experience of my former marriage. To the point that I contacted him and shared this with him and he stated that my words of truth meant so much. Being honest not only established a release, but it put so many blessing in motion. Approximately 24 hours after this discussion with him, I received a monetary blessing and my life completely elevated to a higher level. I know we all have a situation or circumstance that was a class we solicited, not that came up by accident or a coincidence.... Selah.

Remember:

Make you the first in position to love.

Love you first? How? Spend time with the real you every

day – go within and commune with the real you. Listen to

the inner voice of Love within you.

Spend time doing something that makes you happy.

It can be sports, shopping, reading a good book, a walk in

the park and connecting with nature.

Invest into yourself spiritually and as well as naturally.

Spend time with someone or doing something that

challenges you consciously, that causes your mind to evolve

continuously.

Eliminate negative energy from your space.

That can be anything or any person that exerts negative energy. Negative energy is draining and frustrating. Treat yourself! Buy something that you would enjoy having no matter what others might say. Identify something you enjoy doing that brings you peace. A hobby something that takes you into a calm place when you do it. Prosperity follows peace.

We have made a very resolute effort to give you information both spiritual and religious, plus common and learned knowledge and/or sense. We have cited examples and quoted scriptures. We have laid our hearts and lives bare without hesitation. So we want you to receive these engrafted heartfelt words and divine inspirations into your heart, spirit and mind. Allow them to permeate your true self and bring a divine wholeness into your life. Woman YOU are a uniquely crafted being that provide God's presence, both spiritually and physically, in the earth. What other creature has total control over their lives and can influence the lives of others by providing a nurturing warm environment in which to become.

We must take the love of God inside of us and turn it into the love of ourselves and the love of our fellow man and make this a heaven right here on earth. Determine in your heart of hearts to be the *Divine Woman of Design* that God intended and made you to be. It will bless your life and many others also.

So love yourself, you fiercely made *Divine Woman of Design*.

A Place For Your Thoughts...

Notes

Notes

Notes

Notes

Notes

Notes

Notes

Notes

Notes

Notes

Notes

Notes

Notes

Notes

Notes

Notes

Notes

About Kimberly L. Jordan

Kimberly L. Jordan is a native of Chicago, IL and presently resides in the state of Arkansas. Kimberly enjoys inspiring women to be their best Person and live an abundant life that yields happiness. Kimberly spent some years studying the divinity of mankind. She expanded this study along with Margaret Parker in studying the energy of divine feminine.

Kimberly also enjoys designing and making beautiful greeting card creations that touch the souls of people across the United States. Her greeting cards are available in a local Art Gallery. Kimberly is a wife, a Caregiver to her Mother-in-law, and an Aunt.

About Margaret Parker

Margaret Parker is a late blooming writer. Probably late so that she could experience what is presented in this book. Previously she has authored short articles for Newsletters but never anything like this. However, her pastor (who is mentioned in this book) did tell her that one day this would happen. At that time Margaret thought he had lost his mind. But one day Kimberly asked her to be a part of this creation and the rest is history. In addition to writing Margaret enjoys be an integral part of Community theater taking active roles on the Board of Directors and directing plays.

Margaret Parker is a native of Little Rock, AR but has lived in other locations of the U.S. which has enriched her life. She is a mother, grandmother and great grandmother. Looking forward to retirement and living life.

Word Angels
An Imprint of
Butterfly Typeface Publishing

Iris M. Williams
PO Box 56193
Little Rock AR 72215

(501) 823 – 0574

info@butterflytypeface.com

www.butterflytypeface.com

www.ingramcontent.com/pod-product-compliance
Lightning Source LLC
Chambersburg PA
CBHW070014110426
42741CB00034B/1752